The Gift of Baptism

A Handbook for Parents

Tom Sheridan

ACTA Publications
Chicago, Illinois

The Gift of Baptism
A Handbook for Parents
by Tom Sheridan

Tom Sheridan is a writer, journalist, and ordained permanent deacon of the Catholic Church. He has developed and run baptismal preparation programs for many years in the Diocese of Joliet, Illinois, and is the author of *The Gift of Godparents* (ACTA Publications, 1995).

Edited by Thomas R. Artz
Cover design and artwork by Tom A. Wright
Typesetting by Garrison Publications
Printed by Lithocolor Press

Scripture selections are taken from the *New American Bible with Revised New Testament*, copyright © 1986 by the Confraternity of Christian Doctrine. Quotations from the baptismal ceremony are taken from the *Rite of Baptism for Children* copyright © 1969 by the International Committee on English in the Liturgy, Inc.

Copyright © 1996 by Tom Sheridan
Published by ACTA Publications
              Assisting Christians To Act
              4848 N. Clark Street
              Chicago, IL 60640
              800-397-2282

Year 00 99 98 97 96

Printing 7 6 5 4 3 2 1

ISBN: 0-87946-140-3

Library of Congress Number: 96-084007

Printed in the United States of America

Table of Contents

A Very Special Welcome

Dear Parents,

Congratulations on the birth of your child and thank you for taking this first step with your child on a life-long journey of faith.

Baptism is a sacrament of welcome, of acceptance, of challenge, and of opportunity. It welcomes your child into a faith and into a faith community—and welcomes you, your family and friends, and your baby's godparents to share in that same experience.

It's a grand beginning.

Those of us who call ourselves Christians—followers of Jesus, the Christ—welcome you and your child. We may speak different languages, wear different clothes, and have different traditions, but we are the same in our faith. We share our history with Jesus, with the Apostles, and with believers from all generations since.

As a parent, your role at baptism may seem secondary to the role of your child. But that's hardly true. As the parent of a child about to experience the sacrament of baptism, you are blessed with some awesome responsibilities and some tremendous opportunities.

You may never have thought about it in that way. But it's true: You and the godparents you choose are about to make an impact on the faith of a young life. Your role, as you will hear again during your child's baptism, is one which calls you to promise that you will teach your child by word and action about God, faith, and values.

This little book will help you understand and reflect on this sacrament, our shared Christian faith, the baptismal ceremony, the relationship between parent and child and church, and the responsibilities and rewards of being a Christian parent.

God bless you and your child on this lifelong journey of faith.

How Did It All Begin?

Baptism is one of the most important—and most paradoxical—sacraments. For all its popularity (virtually all of Christianity celebrates it in various forms), baptism is perhaps one of the least understood of the sacraments or rites of the church.

Baptism can be a ritual, a social event, a faith-filled moment, a religious milestone, a family tradition, an excuse for a party. And it can be all of these.

Baptism is also a paradox because it is, at the same time, the most personal of sacraments as well as the most communal.

Sometimes parents view their child's baptism as a singular, personal touch from God. They see God's presence as a narrow beam of light from heaven illuminating the child in their arms, while perhaps catching the others present with reflected glow. Other families are more aware of the communal nature of baptism. They recognize the beam to be a floodlight bathing them, the child, and all believing Christians with God's life and love.

In their celebration of baptism, parishes may choose to accentuate either the personal or the communal nature of this sacrament. Celebrating baptism during Sunday Mass, in front of the entire congregation, recognizes the communal nature of the sacrament as the child is greeted and welcomed by everyone.

Other parishes mark the sacrament of baptism in a more personal way— often on a Sunday afternoon—with only family, sponsors (godparents), and close friends present.

Regardless of the number of people present at the ceremony, your child is being baptized into a faith community that celebrates the presence of Jesus Christ and worships together in that place. That is also why baptisms are held in church, rather than in homes, in yards, or down at the local riverbank. The church and your presence at it for this very important Christian milestone is the glue which connects you and your child to the larger community of faithful believers and to their God.

And that, after all, is what baptism is all about.

Through baptism men and women are incorporated into Christ. They are formed into God's people, and obtain forgiveness of all their sins. They are raised from their natural human condition to the dignity of adopted children. They become a new creation through water and the Holy Spirit. They are called, and indeed are, the children of God.

–From Romans 8:15; Galatians 4:5; Council of Trent; John 3:1

There's an old saying that describes a newly baptized infant as "a very early Christian." There's more than a little truth in that. But among the very early Christians—the original ones who lived a long time ago in Palestine, Greece, and the Middle East—baptism was something which almost never included small children.

In the early church, when the Christians were an underground society living in fear of being persecuted, becoming Christian was undertaken rather quietly. An adult who heard the Good News preached by a disciple usually made discreet inquiries about joining the local Christian group. If a candidate seemed sincere, he or she would be instructed in the faith and baptized.

As centuries passed, becoming a Christian wasn't such a dangerous thing anymore. The church was prospering and just about everyone—at least in that part of the world—was Christian. And just like today, Christians were having babies.

9

The church had learned what to do about welcoming adults: It instructed them, accepted them, and baptized them. But when Christians had babies, the church wasn't so sure what to do.

Around the year 400, a bishop named Augustine—we know him today as Saint Augustine—thought and prayed and decided that if these children were going to be raised as Christians they should have the sacramental blessing that goes with being Christian. So the church began baptizing children, placing upon them the seal of the promise of faith. Because they couldn't state their beliefs like adults, it was left to their parents to make the baptismal promises and profession of faith for them.

The tradition of infant baptism continues in the Catholic church and many other Christian faith communities. The parental role remains extremely important. During the baptismal ceremony you are reminded that it is your duty to guide your child in the practice of the faith. That's something you can do well only if you are faithful to God and the Christian community. In that way, baptism is a welcoming event not only for your child, but also for you.

Baptism starts a sacramental initiation that continues with first holy communion (eucharist) and confirmation. For more ideas about how to continue this walk of faith and initiation with your child, see pages 47-52 in this book.

Of course, not all the children presented for baptism are infants. Sometimes they are toddlers, or even older. Although the church encourages that children be baptized as soon as practical, there's no need to feel guilty about not rushing things.

Parents who wait until their child is older can look forward to a different sort of experience. For example, a toddler will have to be told about some of the things which will happen during the ceremony. (Anyone who's tried to pour water over the forehead of an unsuspecting three-year-old understands that.)

Along with learning about their parental role in this sacrament, the parents of toddlers and especially the parents of school-aged children will need to explain the ritual and the reason for baptism in a manner which the child can understand. This could mean purchasing a children's

Bible or a book which explains baptism using age-appropriate words and pictures. It also means involving the child more deeply in the social aspect of this faith-event by letting him or her help plan the party and invite young friends. For more about baptizing an older child, see page 28.

Dearly beloved, these children have been reborn in baptism. They are now called children of God, for so indeed they are. In confirmation, they will receive the fullness of God's Spirit. In holy communion they will share in the banquet of Christ's sacrifice, calling God their Father in the midst of the church.

–Rite of Baptism for Children.

Baptism is not something which magically makes a baby into a Christian. Rather it helps nuture the seeds of faith. The splash of baptismal water or the immersion into a baptismal pool (Yes, more and more Catholic churches do that) and the words said by the priest or deacon during the ceremony are not magic. The church does not believe in a God of magic; it believes in a God who invites, who loves, who forgives.

Baptism helps us affirm that which we already believe—that this child you are presenting to the church is welcomed by God and welcomed, cleansed of all sin, into God's people, the Christian community. This is what the essence of baptism has always been—a welcome by God and the Christian community, an initiation to share the wonders of faith.

From its very beginning, the ritual—and the reality—of baptism has symbolized the joining of a soul to a group of like believers, a community dedicated to following the Creator through Jesus Christ. Baptism is the grand beginning. The rest is up to us. And to God.

It is an awesome and opportunity-filled time.

What Happens during the Baptism?

New parents usually wonder what's going to happen at the baptismal ceremony. Often the first question is, "Omigosh—what am I gonna do at the church?" It's quite a normal reaction.

Baptism presiders—priests and deacons (and, on rare occasions, a bishop)—are usually pretty good at guiding people through the ceremony, especially nervous new parents and godparents. While the basic ritual (ceremony) of baptism is pretty much the same wherever you go, there may be some local differences. That's why it's a good idea to ask the presider or other parish representative ahead of time to explain the procedures used at your parish.

The church teaches that you, the parents, are second only in importance to the child being baptized. Godparents and other family members are important, but not as important as the parents. You are the people to whom your child will turn for guidance. It will be your morals and values that form and shape your child.

Because of this, the church prefers that parents hold their child during the ceremony, even though this may challenge some family and cultural traditions in which the godparent is expected to hold the child. The presider usually will invite godparents to be involved in other ways, such as marking the child with the Sign of the Cross, reading scripture, holding the candle, and standing alongside the parents.

Here's a brief summary of what takes place during the ceremony of baptism.

The Celebration of the Sacrament of Baptism

The baptismal ceremony has four parts:

1. The reception of the child,
2. The celebration of God's Word,
3. The celebration of the water rite,
4. The concluding rite.

Each part has several sections. This is especially true when the baptism is celebrated as a ceremony by itself, usually on a Sunday afternoon. When baptism is celebrated during a Mass, the initial rites may be altered slightly and may take place at the start of or before the Mass, or the entire rite may be celebrated after the homily.

1. The Reception of the Child

The presider greets the congregation and may stress the importance of the family and community gathered as a sign of the community of faithful into which the child is being baptized.

The role of the child's parents and the sponsors is explained.

The parents are asked the name of their child and the reason why they are presenting this child to the church. They answer, "baptism," "entry into God's family," or something similar using their own words.

The parents, sponsors and community are reminded that they accept responsibility for nurturing the child's faith and values.

Do you clearly understand what you have begun here today?

—Rite of Baptism for Children

The welcome into the Christian community is symbolized by marking the child's forehead with the Sign of the Cross. The presider will do this first and then invite the parents and godparents and perhaps all present to make the same sign on the child's forehead.

The Christian community welcomes you with great joy. In its name I claim you for Christ our Savior by the sign of his cross. I now trace the cross on your forehead and invite your parents and godparents to do the same.

—Rite of Baptism for Children

2. The Celebration of God's Word

One or more readings from scripture will be proclaimed. These may be read by the presider or, more often, by a parent, godparent, or other family member.

A homily by the presider helps explain the importance of baptism as a sign of faith.

The presider will offer prayers of the faithful (petitions) for the child, the parents and godparents, the Christian community, and the world. He may invite petitions from parents, godparents, and other members of the congregation.

The presider prays a prayer of healing and anoints the child on the chest. The oil that is used in this anointing is known as the oil of salvation. It reminds us that blessed oil has been an instrument of healing and strength since the time of the early Christian community.

We anoint you with the oil of salvation in the name of Christ our Savior; may he strengthen you with his power, who lives and reigns for ever and ever.

–Rite of Baptism for Children

3. The Celebration of the Water Rite

The presider blesses the water to be used for the baptism.

Parents, godparents, family, and friends are then invited to profess their faith in Jesus Christ who, with them, is to be the lifelong guide for the child being baptized. The presider leads everyone in the renewal of their own baptismal vows.

If your faith makes you ready to accept this responsibility, renew now the vows of your own baptism. Reject sin; profess your faith in Christ Jesus. This is the faith of the church. This is the faith in which this child is about to be baptized.

–Rite of Baptism for Children

The presider baptizes the child with water in the name of the Father, the Son, and the Holy Spirit. Either the water is poured or sprinkled over the forehead, or the child is immersed into a baptismal font.

A candle is lighted from the parish's pascal (Easter) candle and presented to a member of the family, often to one of the godparents.

4. The Concluding Rite

The presider will liberally pour or apply chrism—perfumed oil which is also used in the sacraments of confirmation and ordination —to the top of the child's head as a symbol of service and mission to the people of God.

God the Father of our Lord Jesus Christ has freed you from sin, given you a new birth by water and the Holy Spirit, and welcomed you into his holy people. He now anoints you with the chrism of salvation. As Christ was

17

anointed Priest, Prophet and King, so may you always live as a member of his body, sharing everlasting life.

–Rite of Baptism for Children

The child then receives a white baptismal garment. Some parishes use a small bib-like garment that is placed on the child's breast. If the child has been baptized by immersion, the child is now dressed in a white baptismal gown.

In some parishes, the newly baptized child may be presented to the congregation for a welcoming round of applause. This is sometimes done by the presider, or the parents may be invited to raise their child for all to see.

The ceremony concludes as the community is invited to stand and pray together the Lord's Prayer. The presider then offers a prayer and blessing over the parents, godparents, and the entire congregation.

Why Are Signs and Symbols So Important?

Words are important.

So are signs and symbols.

They can help us understand what is taking place. They can also add meaning to a ceremony or ritual and make it come alive. During the ceremony of baptism, oil and water are the most recognizable symbols. They are ordinary things used in an extraordinary way for this special event.

But there's more to baptism than oil and water. For someone who doesn't understand, the use of such things can be puzzling. So here's a short course on some of the symbols you'll see at your child's baptism.

The Oils. The first anointing, on the child's breast, is with the oil of salvation. It is also known as the oil of baptism or the oil of catechumens. This rite is sometimes omitted, especially when baptism is celebrated during Mass. It recalls the importance of oil in the life of the early church when blessed oil was used for all manner of things: cooking, cleaning, healing, and as an instrument of light and heat. It is used in the first part of the baptism rite as a sign of healing and a sign that the child will be open to the life of the church—the Good News.

There is a second anointing during the baptismal ceremony after the water rite. This time the anointing is done with chrism, the same blessed oil that is used in confirmation and in the ordination of bishops, priests, and deacons.

The Candle. The candle is a sign of the flame of faith and the light of Christ. It is lighted from the church's Easter candle by a parent or godparent and given to the child. It is then suggested that the child burn this candle briefly each year on the anniversary of his or her baptism. It can also be displayed prominently when the child completes the process of Christian initiation at the time of first communion and confirmation.

The White Garment. Most children presented for baptism come dressed in a white gown. In some cases, the gown is an heirloom, or is destined to become one. The white color traditionally recognizes the sinlessness of the child and his or her new life in Christ. As part of the ceremony some parishes place a white, bib-like garment on the child's breast.

When a child is to be baptized by immersion, the parents are advised to bring the child to church in pajamas or casual clothes. After the water rite, the parents and godparents take a few minutes to put on the child's white baptismal gown.

The Water. Clean and clear, the waters of baptism recall the purification bath of the early Christians and their Judaic predecessors. It also memorializes the traditional role water had in the history of our faith, both in the New Testament and in the Hebrew Scriptures (the Old Testament).

The Sign of the Cross. This sign is traced on the forehead of the child as a symbol of the salvation brought about by the suffering and death of Jesus Christ. It also symbolizes the Christian faith that we share and into which the child is being welcomed and initiated.

The essence of baptism remains the birthright of every child—to know the love and touch of God, the welcome of the Christian community and their promise of support.

Life, Love and Baptism

Baptism is a real landmark in our passage of faith. Because we are human—and perhaps especially because we come from a faith in which sharing is so fundamental—baptisms often bring out experiences which cement the divine reality to the human one.

The Kid with the Big Mouth

Everyone who has ever had anything to do with a baptism—whether celebrating it, being a parent or godparent, or just a friend or family member in attendance—has a story to tell.

This is one of those stories.

It all began simply enough. The presider celebrating the baptism, aware that older siblings are often overlooked in an event which stresses the presider, the godparents, and the newborn, thought he had a wonderful idea.

When the time came for the homily, he called all the big brothers and sisters up to the front of the baptismal font. After a few moments of confusion and milling around, there were a number of little boys and girls looking embarrassed and wondering what was going to happen next.

The celebrant talked a little about how everyone there—from parents right on down to the brothers and sisters —was going to teach the little babies being baptized about life, about God, and about a whole lot of things. Then the celebrant asked the children what they were going to teach their brothers and sisters who were being baptized that afternoon.

Some of the kids mumbled. Others had strange bouts of the uncontrollable giggles. It was the sort of things that elementary school teachers—bless 'em all—go through each and every day.

But a few of the more memorable comments went like this:

"I'm going to teach him how to get dirty."

"I'm going to teach her how to make mudpies." (Start in one direction and, it seems, several of the kids will follow like sheep.)

To their credit, however, there were several, "I'm going to teach him how to read" or "to play" or even "to be nice."

And then it happened.

One little girl of about five, the oldest in her family, spoke in clear, bell-like tones that could be heard throughout the church: "I'm gonna teach my little sister to make love."

Imagine that! Right there in church.

Well, as the cliché goes, you could have heard a pin drop. Except for a few nervous shuffles of feet or an occasional self-conscious cough, everyone—and I mean everyone—was silent.

Too bad. The little girl wasn't preaching sexuality; she was proclaiming a basic human truth. That truth is that we must teach each other how to love, how to be lovers, how to be loved.

Her parents, bless them, were rather calm about the whole thing. But they deserved to receive much comment for their daughter's response—all of it positive.

It is a perceptive five-year old who can understand the truth that is at the core of all life. And rather than make her the unfortunate focus of self-conscious chuckles and pokes in each other's ribs, we might all learn a lesson from her.

The celebrant of the baptism, swallowing his own surprise, tried to recover and thank the little lady for her insight.

Yes, baptisms are about learning to love one another.

Beloved, let us love one another, because love is of God; everyone who loves is begotten by God and knows God. Whoever is without love does not know God, for God is love.

—1 John 4: 7-8

# Questions and Answers about Baptism

Everyone has questions about a child's baptism. Some are practical. Others are more theoretical. Here are a few of the most often-asked questions and some honest answers.

Q. God and the church haven't been very important in our lives, but we still want to have our son baptized. Is that OK?

A. Sure. But you must understand that baptism isn't a magical event. It will fall to you as parents to continue the process of initiating your child into faith. Baptism is often an event that brings families back into contact with their religious roots. It can be an opportunity, not just for your child, but for you. As your son becomes older, you will be

The Gift of Baptism

able to teach him the faith and help him prepare for his first communion —and recall for yourself the value of faith, prayer, and the church.

Q. My best friend is not Catholic, but she's a very religious person. Can she still be the godmother for my child?

A. The mission of a godparent is to be a faithful role model for your son or daughter. Since your child is being welcomed into the Catholic faith, the church requires that at least one godparent be a Catholic who has received the sacrament of confirmation. Since most often there are two godparents, it's acceptable for one to be a Catholic and the other to be a member of another Christian community. It is not appropriate, however, for a non-Christian to be a sponsor or godparent.

Q. What is the right time for baptism? We have a toddler. It's not too late for us, is it?

A. No.

The church still teaches that baptism should be celebrated as soon as is practical. But the "hurry-up-before-something-happens" concern is no longer seen as having overriding importance.

The baptism of a toddler or older child brings with it some special graces as well as some special responsibilities. Parents have the obligation to begin teaching their child about baptism and what it means— as well as what will happen at the ceremony. This can be a wonderful time for parents and their child to learn and explore their faith life together.

A. I'm not married. Can my daughter still be baptized?

A. Of course. Presenting your child for baptism acknowledges your commitment to raise her with the knowledge and practice of the Catholic faith. It makes no judgment on you or your child. You are both welcome in the eyes of God.

Q. What's this about baptism by immersion? Is it dangerous?

A. Reinstituting the possibility of celebrating baptism through immersion (plunging the person into a large pool of water) was one of the changes that came from the Second Vatican Council. Long favored by many Protestant denominations, Catholic churches began again in the 1970s to use this richly symbolic action that was prevalent for many centuries in other churches.

The early Christians didn't skimp when it came to using water for the rite of baptism. They often carried it long distances for the celebration. Today, immersion is the ritual the church prefers for baptism, even if sprinkling (pouring water on the child's forehead) is still more common. Immersion is a great sign, signifying in a very real way the death and resurrection that baptism is all about.

Immersion is not submersion. The child is not dunked beneath the water. When baptism is celebrated by immersion, the presider lowers the child — naked — into the baptismal font. The child is usually immersed up to its shoulders three times as the presider announces the words of the ritual: "I baptize you in the name of the Father, and of the Son, and of the Holy Spirit."

Q. One of the baby's aunts want to give our child a gift to commemorate the baptism. What should I suggest?

A. You child's aunt can help create a family heirloom that will reflect the celebration. A Bible makes a wonderful gift. She can give a Bible that your child will be able to read as he or she gets older. There are a number of modern translations available such as the New American Bible and the Good News version. A children's prayer book is also a good idea, as are some of the many music tapes and videos with Bible stories that are now available.

Q. The person we'd like to be our daughter's godfather lives 2,000 miles away. Sadly, there's no way he can be present for the ceremony. What can we do?

A. It might be possible to have a "proxy" godparent. A proxy is a stand-in at the ceremony when the person cannot be present.

It is also possible that all those present will "fill-in" for the missing godparent. In that case the name of the godparent will be noted in the official record of the parish, but there will not be a formal proxy for the absent sponsor.

When a godparent lives some distance, you might encourage the godparent to remain involved as your child is growing up. Suggest that the godparent be present to the child by phone or by letter. Exchanging occasional video taped messages is also a wonderful idea.

Who Can Be a Godparent?

Have you selected your child's godparents yet?

Very likely, how you understand the role of a godparent will determine how you make the selection. Parents bear the obligation of selecting good role models for their children. And there are rules in place to help guide that selection.

Baptism doesn't turn godparents into guardians, legal or otherwise. Yes, it's true that in earlier generations a godparent was often put on permanent faith-guard duty. That meant that if something tragic happened to the child's parents, the godmother would swoop in on the next Greyhound bus, clutch the child to her ample bosom, and spirit the little one off to Sheboygan, or wherever it was that the godmother lived. There, the child would be raised as her own. And, of course, as a Catholic.

Except in some close-knit ethnic communities, most parents make other arrangements for the care of their children in the event of their untimely demise. Generally parents name someone other than the godparent—perhaps the executor of their will—as the child's guardian. The commitment godparents are called to make is a commitment for concern and support, not a commitment for guardianship.

What Are the Qualities of a Good Godparent?

Don't expect the godparents of your child to be perfect ... or saintly, but look for godparents who will be good models of faith and values for your child. Look also for those who will be there to support you in the challenging role of being a faithful Christian parent. A godparent ought to be someone with whom you are comfortable sharing pain as well as joy.

Being a godparent, then, does not require one to be a substitute parent, but it is more than just an honorific title. It is a position that has real value, as a friend and helper both to the child and to his or her parents.

About Those Rules

While some rules about the selection of godparents may vary from diocese to diocese, godparents are generally expected to be over the age of 16 or to have received the sacrament of confirmation. At least one godparent must be Catholic; the other, if not Catholic, must be a believing member of another Christian denomination.

Some parishes expect prospective Catholic godparents to present proof (generally in the form of a letter from their pastor) that they are practicing (active) in their churches. Other parishes don't ask for proof but rely on the judgment of the parents to select people who will be worthy godparents.

A godparent is expected to be a believing Christian because he or she should offer positive Christian values in a world which often lacks for them. After all, if we expect our children to take positive steps in life, then it's our role to show them the right direction.

Sometimes, the best way a godparent can make an impression on the young person is to keep trying to do good, keep trying to make right decisions, keep trying to love God, even when it's not easy. And to keep trying to make the Good News real.

Like our faith, the Good News that Jesus calls each of us to live is neither complex nor magical. It is simply...

To heal the sick. To give sight to the blind. To feed the hungry. To clothe the naked. To welcome strangers. To free the captives. To proclaim the favor of God upon all people.

–based on Matthew 11:5-8

That's not an impossible task for a godparent-to-be. It doesn't take perfection. Only the promise to keep working at it. That's not bad advice for parents, either.

A Godparent's Letter

Dear Lindsey Noel,

You probably didn't feel any different when you awoke this morning. After all, things haven't changed; at least not as far as you can tell. You're still just a few weeks old. You're still mostly concerned with hunger pangs, discomforting diapers, bright lights and large shapes who hover nearby and keep you awake with their cooings and words about how sweet you are.

You really couldn't care less about things like parties or cake.

Or about being welcomed.

I know your Mom and Dad will tell you about it when you're older, but since I'm their friend (and yours) I'd like to add my two-cents' worth.

You couldn't possibly understand what was happening yesterday at church. All you know is that one minute you were warm and dry and cuddled; and the next you were being dunked into a big bowl of water while everyone sang and clapped and thought you were the cutest thing.

Which you were.

It's too bad, though, that you couldn't appreciate the fuss people made over you.

Lindsey, dear unsuspecting Lindsey,

how could you know your friends are welcoming you, making you part of themselves, baptizing you into a relationship with God through the Christian community? How could you know we were sharing you with everything we are, everything we will be?

How could you know we want you to be part of our joys, our laughter, even our struggles? You couldn't know that, at least not now. Someday, though, you will.

And here we didn't even ask if that's what you wanted.

Some people might think that's unfair taking advantage of an unaware infant, no matter how bright-eyed and alert. Or worse, some people might think it's a poor attempt at something magical.

It's neither, of course.

Your baptism really doesn't tell nearly as much about you as it does about your mother and your father, your sisters and your brothers, all your friends and everyone else whose lives will touch yours as you grow. You see, baptism is about community, too.

Lindsey, God loves you. There's no questions about that. By your baptism, we are trying to tell you how much we love you, and how much we love having you as part of the body of Christ with us. We are trying to make you a part of our lives. We want you to know for all time that you belong to a people who believe in the love and the power of God.

There are other, more theological, reasons for your baptism as well, but it'll be a while before you can understand those.

In the meantime, the reality is that we have celebrated the fact that you do belong to our family of faith.

While you wondered what was going on, we celebrated. At the party in your honor, everyone smiled and held you and did all the things people do with babies.

Just as naturally, all the kids ran around. Some played video games. The adults talked about the weather and sports and soap operas. But mostly, it was a community of believing people who came together to say, "Welcome, Lindsey. We're glad you're here."

I think the welcome you were accorded at baptism said it best of all:

Lindsey Noel, you have been called by name by our God from all time, and you have been called by your mom and dad from the earliest stirrings of life. They welcomes you even then as a treasured gift.

It is with a deep sense of joy and an abundance of love and in the name of the entire community that we welcome you as the newest member of our body of Christ. We promise to nurture, support and love you in your growth in the Lord.

And that's a promise you bet we'll keep.

Love,

Your Friend

ow Can I Make My Child's Baptism Special?

Baptism is a special event in the life of your child —and in the life of your family. Here are some suggestions to mark this event and make it a special time of love and grace for all of you.

Understand. Families that take the time to recognize the value and importance of baptism as a faith-centered event as well as a family-centered one will understand the importance of this sacrament in the growth of their child.

Celebrate. Joyously acknowledge this happy event. Celebrate the presence of God in your child's life, and in yours, by continuing to worship together as a family with the faith community you have asked to accept your child

Have a Party. If at all possible, continue the celebration of baptism that began at church with a party in your child's honor. Have ice cream, cake, or whatever. It should not be extravagant—simple and enjoyable is the key. And don't invite the guests only to the party afterward. Invite all of them, even those who are not regular church-goers, to witness the ceremony at your church.

Take Photos. Bring your camera or camcorder. Just be sure to check with the parish to see if they have any rules for such photo-opportunities. Chances are you'll discover they welcome snapshots.

Involve Other Family Members. If you have older children, include them by bringing along their baptismal candles to be lighted from your newest child's candle. If you've misplaced the candles of your older children, replace them now and save them for the future. Ask family members and friends to read the scripture passages or petitions during the ceremony. It will make the ceremony special in their eyes. Involving other relatives by using heirloom baptismal gowns, passed down from generation to generation, is another wonderful idea. If you don't have such an heirloom in your family, create one and begin the tradition now.

Remember. Your child will not recall this moment of faith without your help. Share your feelings, your sense of wonder, your hopes and dreams with your child as he or she grows. When you do these things, you are extending the hand of God. You become an extension of God's love and the welcome of the Christian community.

How Should a Parent Prepare?

By reading this little book you have taken a giant step toward preparing for your child's baptism.

In the days before the ceremony you may want to find a few quiet minutes to reflect on what it means to bring the grace of God to your child in this sacrament and to welcome Christ's life and love into your family in a special way.

To make that easier, this chapter contains the text of four scripture passages that are often used at baptism, along with a brief reflection on each reading. Slowly read the scripture passage and then the reflection. Ask yourself how each reading applies to your life. Then try to make one resolution that will impact your life as a parent in a positive manner. You might even want to write your resolutions on page 63 of this book and look at them once a year on your child's birthday to see how you are doing.

God Welcomes You and Your Child

Thus says the Lord God: I will take you away from among the nations, gather you from all the foreign lands, and bring you back to your own land. I will sprinkle clean water upon you to cleanse you from all your impurities, and from all your idols I will cleanse you. I will give you a new heart and place a new spirit within you, taking from your bodies your stony hearts and giving you natural hearts. I will put my spirit within you

and make you live by my statutes, careful to observe my decrees. You shall live in the land I gave your fathers; you shall be my people, and I will be your God.

–Ezekiel 36:24-28

Home, says a wise old saying, is where, when you go there, they have to let you in .

All of us need to feel welcomed. That's what baptism offers: a sense of welcome, of renewal, of community and relationship. But all of us need assurances of that welcome.

In the Hebrew Scriptures—the Old Testament—we read about the prophet Ezekiel moving about among the people, assuring them that God will always accept them back, always welcome their return, no matter what the circumstances.

To the Hebrews and to us, who sometimes worry about exiling ourselves from the love of God, the prophet's message is a powerful one. God offers to gather us home, to refresh our spirits, to renew our hearts, to become a new creation. Who among us can resist that sort of invitation?

In baptism, God again makes that offer with the assurance that we will always be welcomed home.

We Are United in Christ and We Rejoice

As a body is one though it has many parts, and all the parts of the body, though many, are one body, so also Christ. For in one Spirit we were all baptized into one body, whether Jews or Greeks, slaves or free persons, and we were all given to drink of the one Spirit.

—1 Cor 12:12-13

What does it mean to be "one"? Does it mean that in faith we lose those very important parts of ourselves that make us different from everyone else?

No. Those differences make us who we are, add flavor to our lives and make it possible to have a vibrant and exuberant community. Rather, to be "one" is to share and celebrate those things we have in common.

It means that each of us, through baptism, shares the presence of

God in our lives. Each of us is one part of a larger community called the church. That is one of the reasons why we want our children to be baptized—to make them part of this larger community of believers, the body of Christ.

For the early Christians, there were many things that set them apart from one another. Jew was Jew. Greek was Greek, and most definitely not Jew. Romans were something else entirely. You were who your people were; you were marked by your differences, not united, necessarily, by your connectedness. Slave and free were different; so, of course, were men and women. You could be rich or poor, merchant or soldier, farmer or city-dweller. You could be different in many ways, but you could, at the heart, share Jesus.

This was Christian unity. People who were different in many ways still had God in common. It didn't change them, except on the inside and perhaps, in how they acted toward others. But in a world marked by those external differences, that common unity among Jesus' followers—that "community"—was unique.

Nor is it that much different today. We are still, after all, marked by many of those same differences. We are rich or poor; black, brown, white, or something else. We are men or women; urban, suburban, rural. We are powerful; we are weak. We are professional or laborer. We are many different things.

But when we gather to worship together, we are united into one body, the body of Christ. It is to that Body that we bring our children, and ourselves, in baptism; not in our differences, but in our unity.

Jesus Loves the Little Children ... in All of Us

People were bringing children to him that he touch them, but the disciples rebuked them. When Jesus saw this he became indignant and said to them, "Let the children come to me; do not prevent them, for the kingdom of God belongs to such as these. Amen, I say to you, whoever does not accept the kingdom of God like a child will not enter into it." Then he embraced them and blessed them, placing his hands on them.

–Mark 10:13-16 (Also Matthew 19:13-15; Luke 18:15-17)

This reading (and its companion verses from the Gospels of Matthew and Luke) appears on virtually all lists of recommended scripture passages to be read at baptisms. That's because of the part about Jesus shooing away all those well-meaning but get-in-the-way disciples and gathering the little children to himself.

This passage has a wonderful "Awww, geee" sense about it. But we should not to let it stop there. All of us want our children to be embraced by Jesus, and blessed by him. All of us want them to be welcomed into the kingdom of God. If we're honest about it, though, we want the same things for ourselves, too. But too often, we figure, we've missed out. We think that it's too late for us, but not for our kids. Besides, it's okay to ask Jesus to bless them, but it's embarrassing to ask the same for ourselves. After all, we're not children, are we?

But this reading is not really about our children. It's about the child in us. Jesus does not want us to be childish. Rather, it is the honest, open exuberance of being child-like that the Lord seeks. And that's quite different.

Jesus wants to reach deep inside us and touch the child who lives there. There is a child within us who is open, not skeptical. There is a child within us who is honest, one not so careful to say only the "right things." There is a child within us who loves forthrightly, not out of obligation. There is a child who trusts without fear, who believes in faith, not out of habit.

It is this child—and each of us has one—that Jesus welcomes home and seeks to embrace and bless.

Share the Good News with Everyone

Jesus approached the eleven disciples and said to them, "All power in heaven and on earth has been given to me. Go, therefore, and make disciples of all nations, baptizing them in the name of the Father, and of the Son, and of the Holy Spirit, teaching them to observe all that I have commanded you. And behold, I am with you always, until the end of the age."

–Matthew 28:18-20

Say "church" to someone, and they probably think of rules—about right and wrong, about what to do or not do, what to believe and how, about prayer and about worship.

That someone would be right. But only so far.

That surely is the sense of this scripture reading: Jesus passing on "full authority" to his church and his disciples. Equally strong is the commission for the church and those disciples to pass along that membership to others. That's where baptism comes in and why these words are so often repeated at a baptismal ceremony.

What we sometimes overlook in this reading is the fact that in baptism we become the Lord's modern-day disciples. It becomes our task to spread the Good News in the name of the Father, and of the Son and of the Holy Spirit. That is the mission of all who share in the baptism of Jesus. That is the mission of the child at the font; that is the mission of his or her parents. That is the mission of all present.

Go. Make disciples of all nations.

Scary, isn't it?

The Lord be with you and your child.

By their words and actions, our family and
friends will also instruct our child about the
God in whom we all believe.

What Comes after Baptism?

Baptism is a beginning, not an ending. Baptism doesn't stop when the ceremony is over. Or even after everyone goes home from the party.

Actually, that's when the real stuff of baptism starts.

Throughout the baptismal ceremony, the church stresses the parents' role. That's the way it should be. After all, parents will have a greater, more direct, more tangible effect on their children than the church ever will, even in matters of religion and faith.

During the baptismal ceremony, the priest or deacon will ask the parents if they—along with the godparents—are ready for the task of raising this child in faith and in the spirit of the Good News.

> *You have asked to have your child baptized. In doing so, you are accepting the responsibility of training him (her) in the practice of the faith. It will be your duty to bring her (him) up to keep God's commandments as Christ taught us, by loving God and our neighbor. Do you clearly understand what you are undertaking?*
>
> —Rite of Baptism for Children

Those words, to which you will undoubtedly respond, "Yes!" or "We do!", are the essence of the faith; they are the core of the Gospel. And you, as parents, are to be the primary teachers of your children in matters of faith and values.

Think of your child's baptism as just the beginning. The opportunity for first communion and then confirmation will come along in a few years—faster than you think. These two sacraments, along with baptism, are the sacraments of initiation into the Christian faith.

As part of growing up in the faith and as the necessary preparation for these other sacraments, parents are called upon by the church to share their faith with their child. This is extremely important because this is the faith your children will learn. No amount of religious instruction in a classroom can outweigh the values and expectations and practices a child experiences while being raised.

What Do We Do?

So, how can you prepare your child in the years ahead to be initiated fully into the faith? How can you make your child's baptism become that crucial first step in the faith and the Christian community that the church intends it to be?

It's not that hard, but it does take some thought and preparation. In that sense, it's not unlike the Little League practice, the dance classes, or any of life's other little lessons that you will help your child prepare for and learn. In everything you do or say, you are building the future of your child. And learning about and living one's faith and religion are just one part of a child's growing up.

Here are some suggestions that you can follow as your child grows up.

GOOD IDEA #1: Go to church as a family. Worshipping together makes a powerful impression on young children. It says to them that this "religion thing" must be important; otherwise why would parents do it with them. A child's book about the Mass will help your child to follow along and learn about worship.

GOOD IDEA #2: Take a few minutes to say grace at family mealtimes. Communication with God in prayer is a cornerstone of faith. There are, of course, traditional graces such as:

Bless us, O Lord, and these thy gifts, which we are about

to receive, from thy bounty,
through Christ, our Lord,
Amen.

and

God is Great, God is Good,
let us thank God for our food.
Amen.

But it is also wonderful when families learn to be free enough with each other and with God to make up a thankful grace as they go along. Each family member can add a phrase or individuals can take turns leading the blessing prayer. It can be as simple and straight-forward as:

Thank you, God, for today.
It's been a tough afternoon.
I'm glad I'm home now to
share this meal with the
family you have given me.
Bless this food we share
and the people who share
it with me.

Children have wonderful and vivid imaginations. Often, they are able to express themselves and their faith in very honest and open ways. One child, a sixth-grader, came up with this twist on grace, which became part of his family's traditions:

God is Rad, God is a Dude;
Thank you, God, for this
food.

GOOD IDEA #3: Make prayer a regular part of daily life. Using the free-form mealtime prayers described above encourages children to pray to God in a familiar, personal, conversational way at times other than meals, too. As parents you will also want to help them memorize the traditional prayers in our religious tradition. These include the Our Father, the Hail Mary, and others. Repeating them as part of a bedtime or mealtime ritual with your children helps teach them. But you will also want to encourage them to pray to God in their own words from the depths of their heart.

GOOD IDEA #4: Learn more about the faith. Some of you might be saying, "Wait a minute. I'm not a religious person. I don't know all that stuff. How am I going to help my children grow in the faith?"

Don't panic. Use this as an opportunity to learn along with your child, or perhaps to re-learn something you knew long ago and may have forgotten.

Your parish undoubtedly offers adult education classes. These are a great way to meet people (often other parents learning the same way you are) and become involved in your parish community.

GOOD IDEA #5: Help with your child's religion classes. Most parish-based religious education programs look to parents for assistance with classes, either in helping with planning or even teaching. Don't be intimidated. Such "catechists," as they are called, receive lesson plans, preparation sessions, and support. It may sound frightening at first, but teaching such a class is an experience you and your children will never forget.

GOOD IDEA #6: Be positive about the faith. Make religion important in your home. Most of all, parents should show a positive attitude toward the faith. Realize that the values you demonstrate—from how you treat others to how you show your faith in God—will have a remarkable teaching effect on your children. Kids always watch what you do, even though they may not always do what you tell them. They will grow up with your values and your faith. Are you ready for that?

Good luck!

And trust the Holy Spirit to guide you.

Prayers for Baptism

Prayer of a Child at Baptism
Loving God,

Today, I look to you through the eyes and
through the faith of my parents.

They have brought me here, to this place of baptism,
to celebrate their faith in you as a loving Parent.

They have honored me on this day
by offering to share their faith with me.

And they honor you.

Thank you, Lord, for my parents.

Amen.

Prayer of a Parent at Baptism

Loving God,

You have given me this child.

On this baptism day,
help me to encourage my child's faith.

Help me to foster faith, growth and responsibility
in my child.

Help me to teach, to love, to value,
to honor this child.

But most of all, Lord,
help me always to remember
that this child comes from your love.

Amen.

A Prayer for Godparents

Loving God,

You have given us these people, these friends to be the godparents of our child.

Protect them, preserve them, help them always along the path of life so that they may be present as this small child grows into personhood.

It is a sometimes difficult world, Lord; let these godparents model for our child the love and courage needed to follow your ways. May these godparents help us in our duty as Christian parents, showing by word and example what it means to be part of the body of Christ.

Perhaps most importantly, Lord, let these godparents become our child's friend.

Amen.

A Parent's Prayer for the People Gathered

Creator God, you have gathered around us today a wonderful group of people—loving family and dear friends—to help us celebrate this day of joy and peace.

As our child grows, these are the people who will help us teach our little one about life, about values, about the world. From them, our child will learn about right and wrong.

By their words and actions, our family and friends will also instruct our child about the God in whom we all believe.

We ask you, on this day and on all days, to be with all those gathered here and those who are here in spirit. Help them always to remember that you are an important part of their lives, just as they are an important part of the life of our newly baptized child.

Amen.

A Prayer on the Day of Baptism

This is indeed the day the Lord has made.

God has made it full of warmth and sunshine, whether that warmth and sunshine is in the sky outside or within our hearts.

This is indeed the day the Lord has made.

We welcome this day as a day of rebirth, a day of belonging, a day of commitment for us all.

We celebrate this day, as we will celebrate all the days of this little child's life, secure in the knowledge of God's love.

This is indeed the day the Lord has made.

Let us rejoice in it and be glad.

Amen.

Scripture Readings for Baptism

Matthew 3: 13-17
The baptism of Jesus by John the Baptizer.

Matthew 6: 25-34
Don't worry, God will take care.

Matthew 10: 13-15
Those who welcome you, welcome me.

Matthew 22: 35-40
The first and greatest commandment.

Matthew 28: 18-20
Baptize in the name of the Father, the Son, and the Holy Spirit.

Mark 1: 9-11
The baptism of Jesus.

Mark 3: 31-35
Whoever does the will of God
is my family.

Mark 9: 23
Faith makes everything possible.

Mark 10: 13-16
Let the little children come to me.

Mark 12: 28-31
Love God above all things and
love your neighbor as yourself.

Luke 2: 22-40
The presentation of Jesus
in the temple.

Luke 2: 41-52
The finding of the child Jesus
in the temple.

Luke 11: 9-13
Ask, and you will receive.

John 3: 1-6
Unless you be born again, you will
not enter heaven.

John 4: 14
The water I give provides
everlasting life.

John 4: 5-14
I give Living Water.

John 6: 44-47
No one can come to me unless
the Father calls.

John 7: 37-39
If anyone thirsts, let them
come to me.

John 13: 35-39
Love one another and follow me.

John 14: 23-26
Anyone who loves me will be true
to my word.

John 15: 1-11
I am the vine, you are the
branches; live on in my love.

Acts 2: 42-47
Marks of a Christian community.

Romans 6: 3-5
When we were baptized, we
joined Jesus.

Romans 8: 16-17
How we have become real heirs
of God.

Romans 8: 28-32
We have become more like
God's own.

Romans 8: 38-39
Nothing can separate us
from the love of God.

1 Corinthians 12: 12-13
We are baptized into one Spirit.

1 Corinthians 13: 4-7
Love is patient, kind.

Galatians 3: 26-28
All who are baptized in Christ
have put on Christ.

Ephesians 1: 3-14
God has bestowed on us every
special blessing in heaven.

Ephesians 4: 1-6
One Lord, one faith, one baptism.

Colossians 3: 1-4
Set your heart on higher goals.

Colossians 3: 12-17
You are God's chosen ones.

Colossians 3: 18-25
Rules for a Christian home.

1 Thessalonians 4: 1-3, 7-12
God's will is that you grow
in holiness.

1 Peter 1: 3-5
Let us thank God for all blessings.

1 Peter 1: 22-25
You have been born again.

1 Peter 2: 4-5, 9-10
You are a chosen people.

1 John 3: 1-2
Here is how God looks at us.

1 John 4: 7-16
Let us love one another because
love is of God.

Resolutions for Parents

To celebrate the baptism of my child, I hereby resolve the following:

1. _____

2. _____

3. _____

4. _____

5. _____

Other Resources for Catholic Parents

As a parent of a Catholic child, you might want to learn more about current Catholic beliefs or practices. Here are some other useful resources from ACTA Publications:

Becoming Catholic: Even If You Happen to Be One. A basic introduction to Catholicism for Catholics and non-Catholics alike. 216 pages, $6.95.

Life in Christ. A catechism for adults in traditional question and answer format, newly revised in light of the new universal *Catechism of the Catholic Church*. 316 pages, $4.95.

Daily Meditations (with Scripture) for Busy Moms. A delightful, prayerful meditation and scripture verse for each day of the year. 368 pages, $8.95

Daily Meditations (with Scripture) for Busy Dads. A page-a-day book just for dad. 368 pages, $8.95

The Rosary. A complete recitation of all 15 mysteries of the rosary, accompanied by original music and meditations. Audio cassette, $9.95; compact disk, $12.95; video, $19.95.

Available from bookstores or by calling 800-397-2282.